A Pet's Life

Guinea Pigs

Anita Ganeri

Heinemann Library
Chicago, Illinois

Designed by Richard Parker and Tinstar Design
Limited (www.tinstar.co.uk)
Originated by Dot Gradations
Printed and bound in China by South China Printing
Company

07 06 05
10 9 8 7 6 5 4 3

**Library of Congress
Cataloging-in-Publication Data**
Ganeri, Anita, 1961-
  Guinea pigs / Anita Ganeri.
      v. cm. -- (A pet's life) (Heinemann first library)
Includes bibliographical references (p.   ).
Contents: What is a guinea pig? -- Guinea pig babies --
Your pet guinea pig -- Choosing your guinea pig --
Preparing your cage -- Welcome home -- Guinea pig
play-time -- Feeding time -- Cleaning the cage --
Growing up -- A healthy guinea pig -- Old age.
  ISBN 1-4034-3996-6 (hardcover) -- ISBN 1-4034-4272-
X (pbk.)
  1. Guinea pigs as pets--Juvenile literature. [1. Guinea
pigs. 2. Pets.] I. Title. II. Series.
  SF459.G9G36 2003
  636.9'3592--dc21
                                        2002151594

3829

Acknowledgments
The author and publishers are grateful to the following
for permission to reproduce copyright material: pp. 4,
8, 9, 11, 12, 13, 14, 15, 17, 18, 19, 20, 21, 23, 25 Tudor
Photography; pp. 5, 6, 7, 22, 28, 29 Warren
Photographic/Jane Burton; pp. 10, 24 RSPCA/Angela
Hampton; pp. 16, 26 Chris Honeywell; pp. 27 Mark
Farrell.

Cover photograph reproduced with permission of
Alamy/Maximillian Weinzeir.

The publishers would like to thank Jacque Schultz,
CPDT, Lila Miller, DVM, and Stephen Zawistowski,
Ph.D., CAAB of the ASPCA™ for their assistance in the
preparation of this book.

Also, special thanks to expert reader, Dr. Roberta
Drell, Morton Grove Animal Hospital, Morton Grove,
Illinois.

Some words are shown
in bold, **like this.** You
can find out what they
mean by looking in
the glossary.

Contents

What Is a Guinea Pig?

Guinea pigs are very popular pets. There are many different kinds and colors. Some guinea pigs have short hair. Some guinea pigs have long hair.

A short-haired guinea pig is best for a first-time pet owner.

Here you can see the different parts of a guinea pig's body and what each part is used for.

Ears for hearing.

Fur for warmth.

Small, dark eyes for seeing.

Whiskers for sensing.

Claws for walking and **grooming**.

Long front teeth for **gnawing**.

Guinea Pig Babies

A mother guinea pig usually has about two to four babies in a **litter.** The babies have lots of fur and open eyes.

The baby guinea pigs drink their mother's milk.

The babies are old enough to leave their mother when they are about three weeks old. Then they are ready to become pets.

A female guinea pig can have up to 20 babies a year. It is best to keep males and females apart.

Your Pet Guinea Pigs

Guinea pigs are fun to keep as pets. They can be quite easy to take care of, but you must care for your guinea pig properly.

Your guinea pig will depend on you for all of its needs.

Your guinea pig needs food and water every day. If you are going on vacation, ask a friend or neighbor to look after your pet.

Write a list of what your friend should do and leave it by the guinea pig cage.

Choosing Your Guinea Pigs

Animal shelters often need good homes for guinea pigs. You can also buy guinea pigs from pet stores or **breeders.**

Guinea pigs like company. Choose two males or two females from the same **litter.**

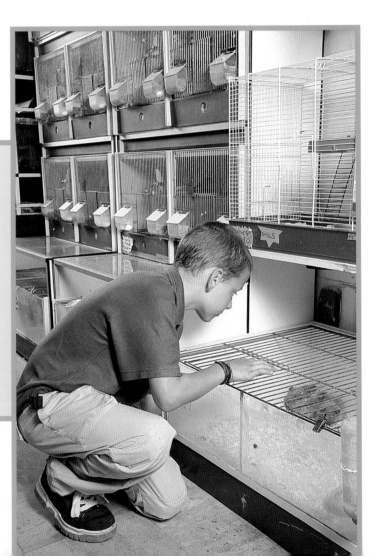

Pick a chubby guinea pig with a shiny coat. Check that its ears and eyes are clean, and that its teeth are not too long.

A healthy guinea pig will be lively and interested in you.

Your Guinea Pigs's Cage

Your guinea pigs need a large cage to live in. Put a layer of unscented hardwood **shavings** on the floor, and a clean pile of hay for bedding.

Do not use a cage with a wire floor. This will hurt your guinea pigs's feet.

Keep the cage in a warm place inside your house. Be sure it is safe from loud noises and other pets.

For two guinea pigs, the house should measure at least 18 inches (46 cm) high, 24 inches (61 cm) wide, and 3 to 6 feet (1 to 2 m) long.

Welcome Home

You can bring your guinea pigs home in a small cardboard box. Make sure the box has holes in it so that your guinea pigs get some air.

At home, put your guinea pigs in their cage. Leave them alone for a few hours to settle in.

Guinea pigs are quite shy. Be gentle when you pick your pet up. Put one hand under its bottom and the other hand around its shoulders.

Stroke your guinea pig gently and talk to it softly.

15

Play Time

Guinea pigs need lots of space to play and exercise. They like to use tubes to run through. Guinea pigs do not jump or climb.

Guinea pigs need a safe area to run around and explore.

Guinea pigs also love to play hide and seek. Put some pillows, stuffed animals, or other objects on the floor for your pet to explore and hide behind.

Check all toys for small pieces that can hurt your guinea pig.

Feeding Time

You can buy guinea pig food from a pet store. Guinea pigs like chopped fresh fruit and vegetables. They also need fresh hay.

Your guinea pig needs lots of **Vitamin C.** It can get this from kale, parsley, beet greens, spinach, red and green peppers, broccoli, tomatoes, kiwi, and oranges.

You should feed your guinea pigs every morning and evening. Put the food in a heavy bowl that will not tip over. Hay and water should be available at all times.

Make sure that your guinea pig has fresh drinking water every day. Put it in a water bottle.

Cleaning the Cage

You can help to keep your guinea pig healthy by keeping its cage clean. Remove any wet bedding, old food, and **droppings** every day.

You also need to wash out the water bottle and food bowl daily.

Once a week, empty the cage and give it a good cleaning. Put in some fresh unscented hardwood **shavings** and bedding. Wash your hands when you are done.

At least four times a year, give the house a complete scrubbing. Allow it to dry before you put your pet back in.

21

Growing Up

Guinea pigs grow up quickly. When a male guinea pig is full grown, it will weigh about two pounds (1 kilogram). Female guinea pigs are a little smaller.

Male guinea pigs are bigger than females.

Guinea pigs like to make noise. They squeak, tweet, chatter, and whistle. You will learn to understand what your guinea pig is talking about.

If your guinea pig whistles, it can mean that it is hungry, thirsty, or happy to see you.

Healthy Guinea Pigs

Your guinea pig will stay healthy if you take care of it. Your guinea pig should go to the **veterinarian** every six months for a checkup.

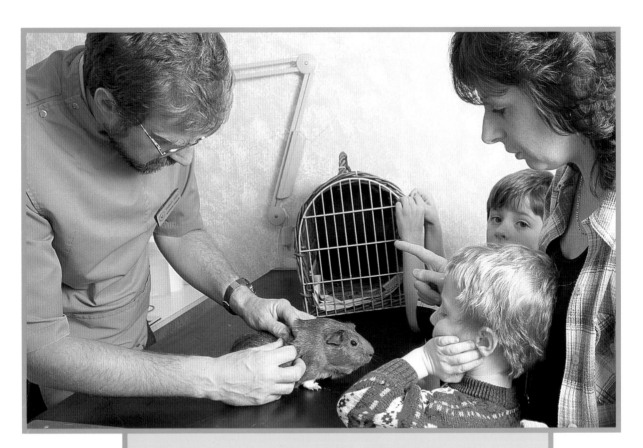

If your pet looks sick, take it to a veterinarian as soon as possible.

A guinea pig's front teeth and claws can grow too long. Give your pet a wooden **gnawing** block to wear its teeth down. A veterinarian can trim its claws.

If your guinea pig's teeth grow too long, it will not be able to eat properly.

Old Age

If you look after your guinea pigs, they may live for up to seven years. As they get older, check them every day to make sure that they are healthy.

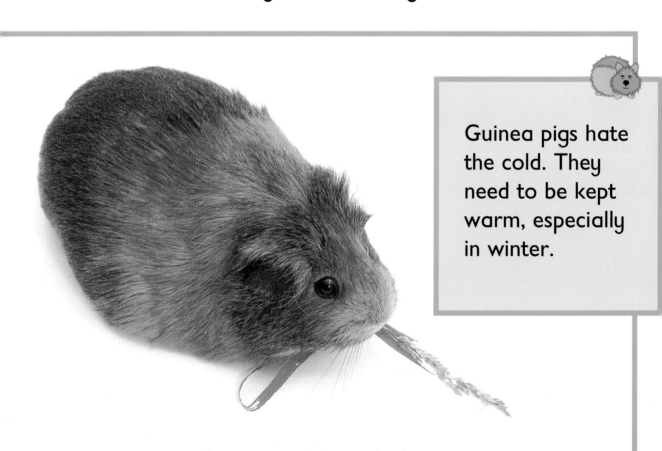

Guinea pigs hate the cold. They need to be kept warm, especially in winter.

Older guinea pigs still need to be cared for every day. They will still enjoy being held and cuddled.

Caring for your guinea pigs will help you learn how to treat animals properly.

Useful Tips

- Always wash your hands before and after touching your pets.

- Guinea pigs **groom** themselves. But you need to brush long-haired guinea pigs every day to stop their fur from getting tangled. Use a soft toothbrush or a baby's hairbrush.

- If your pet holds its head to one side and cannot walk in a straight line, it may have an ear **infection.** Take your pet to a **veterinarian.**

- If your guinea pigs start pulling out each other's hair, it means that they are bored. Make sure that they get plenty of exercise.

- Do not let guinea pigs run around your house alone. They may get hurt.

Fact File

- Wild guinea pigs live in South America.

- Guinea pigs are named after Guiana, the South American country in which they were found.

- Guinea pigs are rodents. They belong to the same group of animals as hamsters, squirrels, mice, and rats.

- Male guinea pigs are called boars and females are called sows, just like real pigs.

- Adult guinea pigs need dry food and hay every day, plus a small amount of fresh fruit and vegetables.

- Guinea pigs can catch colds from humans.

Glossary

animal shelter place where lost or unwanted animals live until they are given new homes

breeder someone who raises animals

communication how animals talk to each other and to you

dropping waste from the body

gnaw chew and bite

groom gently brush and clean your guinea pig's fur. Guinea pigs also groom themselves.

infection sickness

litter group of guinea pig babies

shaving thin slice or strip of wood

vitamin C nutrition from food which guinea pigs need to stay healthy

veterinarian doctor who cares for animals

More Books to Read

An older reader can help you with these books.

Blackaby, Susan. *A Guinea Pig for You: Caring for Your Guinea Pig*. Minneapolis, Minn.: Picture Window Books, 2003.

Carroll, David. *The ASPCA Complete Guide to Pet Care*. New York: Dutton/Plume, 2001.

Miller, Michaela. *Guinea Pigs*. Chicago: Heinemann Library, 1998.

Nelson, Robin. *Pet Guinea Pig*. Minneapolis, Minn.: Lerner Publishing Group, 2002.

Royston, Angela. *Guinea Pig*. Madison, Wis.: Turtleback Books, 1998.

Royston, Angela. *Life Cycle of a Guinea Pig*. Chicago: Heinemann Library, 1998.

A Note from the ASPCA™
Pets are often our good friends for the very best of reasons. They don't care how we look, how we dress, or who our friends are. They like us because we are nice to them and take care of them. That's what being friends is all about.

This book has given you information to help you know what your pet needs. Learn all you can from this book and others, and from people who know about animals, such as veterinarians and workers at animal shelters like the ASPCA™. You will soon become your pet's most important friend.

Index